Perspectives

Being Brave
What Does It Mean?

Series Consultant: Linda Hoyt

Flying Start
to Literacy®

Contents

Introduction

Being brave: What does it mean?

What does being brave look like? A firefighter rescuing someone from a burning building? A skydiver jumping out of a plane?

Being brave can mean something different for everyone. It can mean standing up for something you believe in, even if you're the only one who does so. And being brave can mean overcoming a fear – doing something for the first time even though you're scared.

What does being brave mean to you?

Emergency!

In an emergency, you can feel scared – and
sometimes, it's hard to know what to do.
It's important to stay calm and be brave,
even if you are frightened.

What would you do?

Cool in a Crisis

Brave ten-year-old saves grandmother

Grace Saunders is just ten years old, but last Saturday, she did something extraordinary. She saved her grandmother's life.

Grace and her grandmother, 68-year-old Maria Martinez, were about to eat lunch at home when Maria tripped on a step and fell.

"My grandma looked like she was sleeping," said Grace. "I couldn't wake her, but I could see that she was breathing. No one else was home and I knew we needed help."

Grace called 000.

"Grace was very calm," said Robin Van Bergen, the operator who took Grace's call. "She was able to hide her fear and follow my instructions until the ambulance arrived."

Maria is now back to good health and is proud of Grace.

"She was so brave! She definitely saved my life!"

Speak out!

Hear what these students have to say about the times they were brave.

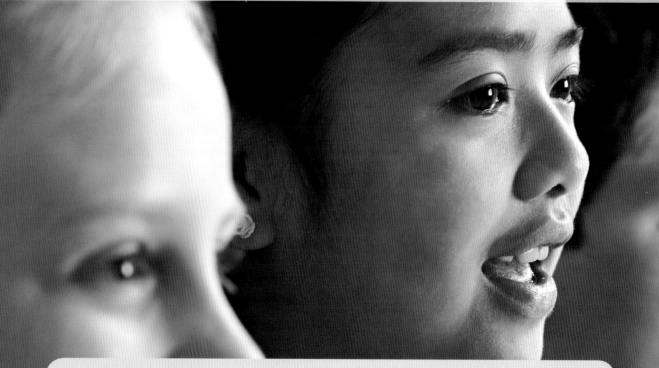

I auditioned for a role in the school play. I was worried that if I got the role, I would forget the script. But I still wanted to do it. I felt nervous before the audition. But at the audition, I didn't feel so bad. Afterwards, I felt relieved!

When I have to get an injection, I must be brave because I hate injections. But I tell myself that the injection is stopping me from getting sick, so it's all for the best.

I had to learn to be brave when I saw a spider. My dad helped me. He showed me how to walk past the spider without disturbing it – that took a long time. It's silly to be scared of such a little creature, so I'm glad I was brave.

When I was younger, I wanted to jump from a big plank onto another big plank. There was a big gap, and I knew it was tricky for me. But then I saw a big kid do it, so I wanted to copy him. And I did!

Trying new things

Would you do this?
How would you feel?

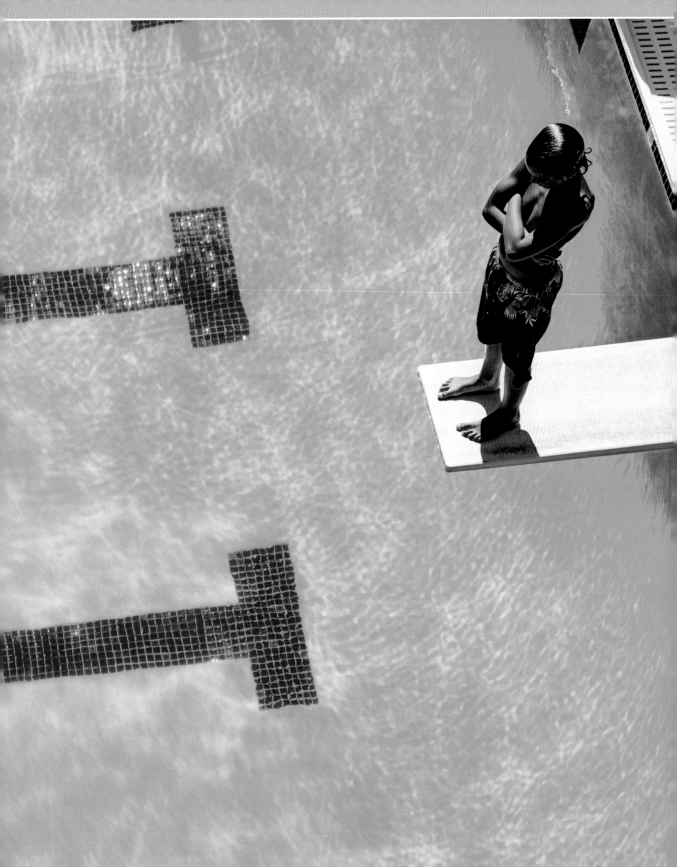

Taking a stand

Sam has two very good friends, but his two friends don't get along.

If one of your friends is being mean to another friend, what should you do?

Last Monday

Oli and I were playing soccer at the park when Tom turned up.

"Hey, Sam. Hey, Oli," said Tom. "Can I play?"

"Okay," I said. "Do you want to be goalkeeper?"

"Sure!" said Tom.

Oli didn't say anything. But when the game started, he said mean things every time Tom made a mistake. Suddenly, Tom stopped playing and walked away without even saying goodbye. I thought this was a bit weird, but I didn't say anything.

Friday

Tom asked me to spend the night at his house. While we were playing video games, I asked him why he had left Oli and me without saying goodbye the other day. Tom said, "No reason," and he didn't seem to want to talk about it.

But later that night, as I was trying to fall asleep, I heard a strange whimpering sound.

"Tom, is that you?"

In a shaky voice, he said, "Yes."

"What's wrong?"

"It's Oli," he said. "He's always so mean to me at school."

I told Tom that on Monday I would tell Oli to stop being so mean to him. That made him feel better.

Sunday

I am worried about tomorrow because if I say something to Oli, I might lose him as a friend.

And I'm worried that if I don't say something, I'll lose Tom as a friend. So I don't know what to do.

Monday

At lunchtime, I walk over to the soccer field. There are about ten kids playing soccer. Tom takes a shot at the goal and misses horribly.

Oli shouts out, "How could you miss that? Maybe you're not as great at soccer as you think you are!" And everyone starts laughing.

My stomach feels like there are a million butterflies in it. I'm scared. I want to say something, but I'm not sure what. But then I think: What would I want Tom to say if I was in his position?

I call out to Oli, "That's mean. Why would you say that?"

"It was a joke. Relax, Sam," says Oli. He looks around, expecting to see the crowd laughing. But no one is smiling. Oli looks unsure about what to do next.

"I was only joking, Tom," says Oli. "I won't do it again."

"It's okay," says Tom.

Maybe Oli was only joking, but he did hurt Tom's feelings. If he does it again, I will tell my teacher.

I'm glad I was brave and said something. Hopefully now Oli will think about Tom's feelings before saying something mean.

How to write about your opinion

State your opinion

Think about the main question in the introduction on page 4 of this book. What is your opinion?

Research

Look for other information that you need to back up your opinion.

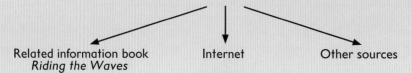

Related information book *Riding the Waves*	Internet	Other sources

Make a plan

Introduction

How will you "hook" the reader to get them interested?

Write a sentence that makes your opinion clear.

List reasons to support your opinion.

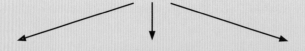

Support your reason with examples.	Support your reason with examples.	Support your reason with examples.

Conclusion

Write a sentence that makes your opinion clear. Leave your reader with a strong message.

Publish

Publish your writing.

Include some graphics or visual images.